P9-CAS-448

Photo by Joan Marcus

A scene from the Westside Arts Theatre production of "The Cryptogram." Set design by John Lee Beatty.

THE
CRYPTOGRAM

BY DAVID MAMET

★

★

DRAMATISTS
PLAY SERVICE
INC.

THE CRYPTOGRAM
Copyright © 1995, David Mamet

All Rights Reserved

CAUTION: Professionals and amateurs are hereby warned that performance of THE CRYPTOGRAM is subject to a royalty. It is fully protected under the copyright laws of the United States of America, and of all countries covered by the International Copyright Union (including the Dominion of Canada and the rest of the British Commonwealth), and of all countries covered by the Pan-American Copyright Convention, the Universal Copyright Convention, the Berne Convention, and of all countries with which the United States has reciprocal copyright relations. All rights, including professional/amateur stage rights, motion picture, recitation, lecturing, public reading, radio broadcasting, television, video or sound recording, all other forms of mechanical or electronic reproduction, such as CD-ROM, CD-I, DVD, information storage and retrieval systems and photocopying, and the rights of translation into foreign languages, are strictly reserved. Particular emphasis is placed upon the matter of readings, permission for which must be secured from the Author's agent in writing.

The stage performance rights in THE CRYPTOGRAM (other than first class rights) are controlled exclusively by the DRAMATISTS PLAY SERVICE, INC., 440 Park Avenue South, New York, NY, 10016. No professional or non-professional performance of the Play (excluding first class professional performance) may be given without obtaining in advance the written permission of the DRAMATISTS PLAY SERVICE, INC., and paying the requisite fee.

Inquiries concerning all other rights should be addressed to Rosenstone/Wender, 3 East 48th Street, New York, NY, 10017. Attn: Howard Rosenstone.

SPECIAL NOTE

Anyone receiving permission to produce THE CRYPTOGRAM is required (1) to give credit to the Author as sole and exclusive Author of the Play on the title page of all programs distributed in connection with performances of the Play and in all instances in which the title of the Play appears for purposes of advertising, publicizing or otherwise exploiting the Play and/or a production thereof. The name of the Author must appear on a separate line, in which no other name appears, immediately beneath the title and in size of type equal to 50% of the largest, most prominent letter used for the title of the Play. No person, firm or entity may receive credit larger or more prominent than that accorded the Author; and (2) to give the following acknowledgments on the title page of all programs distributed in connection with performances of the Play:

THE CRYPTOGRAM was first produced at the Ambassadors Theatre, London, on June 29, 1994, by Frederick Zollo, Nicholas Paleologos, Gregory Mosher, Susan Gallin, David Richenthal, Suki Sandler, and Frank and Woji Gero.

The American premiere of THE CRYTOGRAM was produced on February 8, 1995, by the American Repertory Theatre, Boston, Massachusetts, as part of their New Stages '95 Series.

THE CRYPTOGRAM was produced at the Westside Arts Theatre in New York City on March 28th, 1995, by Frederick Zollo, Nicholas Paleologos, Gregory Mosher, Jujamcyn Theatres, Herb Alpert, and Margo Lion.

This play is dedicated to
Gregory Mosher

THE CRYPTOGRAM was first produced by Frederick Zollo, Nicholas Paleologos, Gregory Mosher, Susan Gallin, David Richenthal, Suki Sandler and Frank and Woji Gero, and presented at the Ambassadors Theatre, in London, England, on June 29, 1994. It was directed by Gregory Mosher; the set design was by Bob Crowley and the lighting design was by Rich Fisher. The cast was as follows:

DONNY .... Lindsay Duncan
DEL .... Eddie Izzard
JOHN .... Danny Worters/Richard Crowley

THE CRYPTOGRAM received its American premiere at the American Repertory Theatre, in Boston, Massachusetts, as part of their New Stages '95 Series, by special arrangement with Frederick Zollo, Nicholas Paleologos and Gregory Mosher, on February 8, 1995. It was directed by David Mamet; the set design was by John Lee Beatty; the costume design was by Harriet Voyt; the lighting design was by Dennis Parichy and the stage manager was Carol Dawes. The cast was as follows:

DONNY .... Felicity Huffman
DEL .... Ed Begley, Jr.
JOHN .... Shelton Dane

THE CRYPTOGRAM was produced by Frederick Zollo, Nicholas Paleologos, Gregory Mosher, Jujamcyn Theaters, Herb Alpert and Margo Lion at the Westside Arts Theatre, in New York City, on March 28, 1995. It was directed by David Mamet; the set design was by John Lee Beatty; the costume design was by Harriet Voyt and the lighting design was by Dennis Parichy. The cast was as follows:

DONNY .... Felicity Huffman
DEL .... Ed Begley, Jr.
JOHN .... Shelton Dane

Last night when you were all in bed
Mrs. O'Leary left a lantern in her shed

Camping song

CHARACTERS

DONNY — A woman in her late thirties
DEL — A man of the same age
JOHN — Donny's son, around ten

The action takes place in Donny's living room in 1959.

ONE
One evening.

TWO
The next night.

THREE
Evening, one month later.

THE CRYPTOGRAM

ACT ONE

A living room. One door leading off to the kitchen, one stair-case leading up to the second floor. Evening. Del is seated on the couch. John comes downstairs dressed in his pajamas.

JOHN.   I couldn't find 'em.

DEL.   ... couldn't find 'em.

JOHN.   No.

DEL.   What?

JOHN.   Slippers.

DEL.   Yes?

JOHN.   They're packed.

DEL.   ... slippers are packed.

JOHN.   Yes.

DEL.   Why did you pack them?

JOHN.   Take them along.

DEL.   How are you going to use your slippers in the woods.

JOHN.   To keep my feet warm.

DEL.   Mmm.

JOHN.   I shouldn't of packed them?

DEL.   Well, put something on your feet.

JOHN.   What?

DEL.   Socks.

JOHN.   Put something on my feet now.

DEL.   Yes.

JOHN.   "As long as I'm warm."

DEL.   That's correct.

JOHN.   I have 'em. *(Produces socks. Starts putting them on.)*

DEL.   That's good. Think ahead.

JOHN.   Why did you say "why did you pack them?"

DEL. I wondered that you'd take them with.

JOHN. Why?

DEL. Out in the Woods?

JOHN. No, but to wear in the Cabin.

DEL. ... that's right.

JOHN. Don't you think?

DEL. I do.

JOHN. I know I couldn't wear them in the woods.

DEL. No. No. That's right. Where were we?

JOHN. Issues of sleep.

DEL. ... is ...

JOHN. Issues of sleep.

DEL. No. I'm sorry. You were quite correct. To take your slippers. I spoke too quickly.

JOHN. That's all right.

DEL. Thank you. *(Pause.)* Where were we? Issues of Sleep.

JOHN. And last night either.

DEL. Mm...?

JOHN. ... I couldn't sleep.

DEL. So I'm told. *(Pause.)*

JOHN. Last night, either.

DEL. Fine. What does it mean "I could not sleep"?

JOHN. ... what does it mean?

DEL. Yes. It means nothing other than the meaning you choose to assign to it.

JOHN. I don't get you.

DEL. I'm going to explain myself.

JOHN. Good.

DEL. A "Trip," for example, you've been looking forward to.

JOHN. A trip. Yes. Oh, yes.

DEL. ... absolutely right.

JOHN. ... that I'm excited.

DEL. ... who wouldn't be?

JOHN. *Anyone* would be.

DEL. That's right.

JOHN. ... to go in the *Woods...*?

DEL. Well. You see? You've answered your own question.

JOHN. Yes. That I'm excited.

8

DEL. I can't blame you.

JOHN. You can't.

DEL. No. Do you see?

JOHN. That it's natural.

DEL. I think it is.

JOHN. Is it?

DEL. I think it absolutely is. To go with your *father*...?

JOHN. Why isn't he home?

DEL. We don t know.

JOHN. ... because it's something. To go out there.

DEL. I should say.

JOHN. In the Woods...?

DEL. ... I hope to tell you.

JOHN. Well, you *know* it is.

DEL. That I do. And I will tell you: older people, too. Grown people. You know what they do? The night before a trip?

JOHN. What do they do?

DEL. Well, many times *they* cannot sleep. *They* will stay up that night.

JOHN. They will?

DEL. Oh yes.

JOHN. Why?

DEL. They can't sleep. No. Why? Because their minds, you see, are full of thoughts.

JOHN. What are their thoughts of?

DEL. Their thoughts are of two things.

JOHN. Yes?

DEL. Of what they're *leaving*.

JOHN. ... yes?

DEL. And what they're going *toward*. (Pause.) Just like you.

JOHN. ... of what they're leaving ...

DEL. ... mmm ... (Pause.)

JOHN. How do you know that?

DEL. Well, you know, they say we live and learn.

JOHN. They do?

DEL. That's what they say. And I'll tell you *another* thing ...
(A crash is heard offstage. Pause.)

9

DONNY. *(Offstage.)* … I'm all right

DEL. … what?

DONNY. *(Offstage.)* I'm all right …

DEL. … did …

DONNY. *(Offstage.)* What? Did I what?

DEL. Are you …

DONNY. *(Offstage.)* What? I've spilt the tea.

DEL. What?

DONNY. *(Offstage.)* I spilled the tea.

DEL. Do you want help?

DONNY. *(Offstage.)* What?

JOHN. Do you want help he said.

DONNY. *(Offstage.)* No.

DEL. You don't? *(To John.)* Go help your mother.

DONNY. *(Offstage. Simultaneous with "mother.")* … I'm all right. I'm all right. *(To self.)* Oh, hell …

DEL. What did you do?

DONNY. *(Offstage.)* What?

DEL. … what did you do …

DONNY. I broke the pot, I broke the teapot. I'm all right. I broke the teapot. *(Pause.)*

DEL. *(To John.)* Well, there you go … a human *being* …

JOHN. … yes?

DEL. … cannot conceal himself.

JOHN. That's an example?

DEL. Well, hell, look at it: anything. When it is *disordered*, any, um, "Change," do you see…?

JOHN. What is the change?

DEL. The trip.

JOHN. She ain't going.

DEL. No of course she's not. But *you* are. And your father is. It's an upheaval.

JOHN. It's a minor one.

DEL. Who is to say? *(Pause.)*

JOHN. But did *you* feel that?

DEL. Did I…?

JOHN. Yes.

DEL. Feel what?

10

JOHN.　Last week.

DEL.　Feel. Last week.

JOHN.　Thoughts on a trip.

DEL.　... Did I...?

JOHN.　When you took *your* trip.

DONNY.　*(Offstage.)* It's going to be a minute.

JOHN.　... when you took your trip.

DONNY.　*(Offstage.)* ... hello...?

DEL.　We're all right.

DONNY.　*(Offstage.)* The tea is going to be a minute.

JOHN.　We're all right in here.

DONNY.　*(Entering.)* I've put the ... why aren't you asleep.

DEL.　... did I feel "pressure"?

DONNY.　... John...?

JOHN.　Yes.

DONNY.　Why aren't you asleep?

DEL.　Before my trip. No.

JOHN.　No. Why?

DEL.　Because, and this is important. Because people differ.

DONNY.　What are you doing down here?

DEL.　We're talking.

JOHN.　... I came down.

DEL.　*(To Donny.)* I'm sorry. Are you all right?

DONNY.　What? I dropped the teapot. What are you *doing* down ...

JOHN.　We're talking.

DEL.　He came down, and I began a conversation.

DONNY.　All right, if you began it.

DEL.　I did.

DONNY.　*(Sighs.)* We're going to have tea, and then you go upst.... Where are your slippers?

JOHN.　Packed.

DONNY.　They're packed.

JOHN.　For the trip.

DONNY.　And then you go upstairs and you go to sleep.

JOHN.　I want to wait 'til my father comes home.

DONNY.　Well, yes, I'm sure you do. But you need your sleep. And if you don't get it, you're not going on the trip.

11

JOHN. Will he be home soon?

DONNY. Yes. He will.

JOHN. Where is he?

DONNY. I don't know. Yes, I do, yes. He's at the Office. And he'll be home soon.

JOHN. Why is he working late?

DONNY. I don't know. We'll find out when he comes home, John. Must we do this every night?

JOHN. I only want ...

DEL. Do you know what?

JOHN. I didn't want to upset you, I only ...

DEL. ... could I...?

JOHN. I only ...

DEL. *(Simultaneous with "only.")* Could I make a suggestion? *(To John.)* Why don't you busy yourself?

DONNY. He has to sleep.

DEL. ... but he's not *going* to sleep. He's ...

JOHN. That's right.

DONNY. ... one moment.

JOHN. ... If I had something to *do* ...

DONNY. *(Simultaneous with "do.")* No. You're absolutely right.

JOHN. ... something to do. If I had *that* ...

DONNY. All right.

DEL. Are you packed?

JOHN. I'm all packed.

DEL. ... well ...

JOHN. I, I My *Father* isn't packed, his ...

DONNY. No ...

JOHN. ... I could pack *his* stuff.

DONNY. No, no, I'll tell you what you could do.

JOHN. What?

DONNY. Close up the attic.

JOHN. ... close it up?

DONNY. Neaten it up. Yes.

JOHN. Is it disturbed?

DONNY. Mmm.

JOHN. Why?

DONNY. ... after my "rummaging."

disconnected + interrupted conversations

12

JOHN. All right.

DONNY. ... and ...

JOHN. ... all right.

DONNY. See if you find any things up there.

JOHN. Things.

DONNY. ... you might need to take.

JOHN. ... things I might need to take up.

DONNY. Mm.

JOHN. Or that *he* might need.

DONNY. That's right.

JOHN. ... or that you forgot.

DONNY. Yes.

JOHN. To pack.

DONNY. Yes. Would you do that?

JOHN. Of course.

DONNY. Thank you, John.

DEL. Thank you.

DONNY. And perhaps you'd put on some clothing.

JOHN. Good.

DONNY. Very good. Off you go then.

JOHN. I will.

DEL. "My blessings on your House."

JOHN. That's what the Wizard, said. *book references*

DEL. That's right. ?

JOHN. "And mine on yours."

DEL. "Until the whale shall speak."

JOHN. "Until the Moon shall Weep." Mother?

DONNY. I don't remember it ... *(Pause.)*

JOHN. You don't remember it? *(Pause.)*

DEL. Well then, John. All right then. Off you go to work.

JOHN. *(Exiting.)* I will.

DEL. Off you go. *(Pause.)*

DONNY. No. I don't understand it.

DEL. Well ...

DONNY. No.

DEL. He has trouble sleeping.

DONNY. Mm. No.

DEL. That's his nature.

DONNY. Is it?

DEL. Children …

DONNY. No. You see. It's grown into this minuet. Every night …

DEL. Well, yes. But this is *special*, he …

DONNY. No, No. He always has a reason. Some … every night …

DEL. Yes. Granted. But a Trip to the Woods …

DONNY. … he …

DEL. … with his Dad…? It's an *event*. I think. What do I know? But, as his *friend* …

DONNY. … yes …

DEL. … as his *friend* …

DONNY. Yes. Yes. He Always has a Reason.

DEL. Yes, but I'm saying, in *spite* of … *I* don't know. I don't mean to intrude … but good. But *Good*. One sends him up to the Attic …

DONNY. Oh.

DEL. And that's "it." That the solution.

DONNY. Oh. Oh …

DEL. To, um … to, um what is the word…?

DONNY. Look what I found.

DEL. To um … not "portray" … to um …

DONNY. Look what I found.

DEL. "Participate." That's the word. Is that the word? No. To, um …

DONNY. Del. Shut up.

DEL. To um …

DONNY. *(Simultaneous with "To.")* Shut up. Look what I found up in the attic. *(She goes to a side table and brings back a small framed photograph and hands it to Del.)*

DEL. *(Pause.)* When was this taken …

DONNY. *(Simultaneous with "taken.")* When I was packing for the trip.

DEL. *(Simultaneous with "trip.")* Mmm…. No. When was this taken?

DONNY. Isn't it funny? Though? The things you find? *(Pause.)*

14

DEL.   Huh ...

DONNY.   What?

DEL.   I don't understand this photograph. *(Pause.)*

DONNY.   What do you mean? *(John comes down onto the landing.)*

JOHN.   Which coat? That's what I forgot. To pack my coat.

DONNY.   *(To Del.)* Which coat?

JOHN.   That's what was on my mind.

DONNY.   Which coat should he take?

DEL.   *(Looking up from the photograph.)* Mm? When were you up there?

DONNY.   Where?

DEL.   Up in the attic?

DONNY.   *(Simultaneous with "attic.")* In the attic today, cleaning up.

DEL.   *(Of photo. Simultaneous with "up.")* ... this is the damnedest thing ...

DONNY.   *Isn't it...?*

DEL.   When, when could this have been taken?

DONNY.   And I found that old *Lap* robe.

DEL.   The lap robe ...

DONNY.   The *stadium* blanket we ...

JOHN.   Which coat?

DONNY.   Which?

JOHN.   How cold is it up there yet?

DEL.   ... a lap robe ...

DONNY.   The *stadium* blanket.

JOHN.   How cold was it last week? Del?

DONNY.   Just bring your regular coat.

JOHN.   My blue coat?

DONNY.   The melton coat?

JOHN.   What's melton?

DONNY.   The blue coat. Your fabric coat.

JOHN.   The *wool* one?

DONNY.   *(To Del.)* Is it too cold for that?

DEL.   No.

DONNY.   Then take it.

JOHN.   My *blue* coat.

DONNY. Yes.

JOHN. Do I have any sweaters left?

DONNY. Up there?

JOHN. Yes.

DEL. I think so.

DONNY. I'm sure that you do.

JOHN. You think so?

DEL. They'd be in your bureau.

JOHN. And, the fishing stuff. Is it there?

DONNY. The fishing stuff. They brought back. Last week, John. It's all ...

JOHN. ... they brought it back.

DONNY. Yes. It's up in the attic ...

JOHN. *(Simultaneous with "attic.")* You should have left it at the Cabin.

DONNY. It's in the attic. You'll see it up there.

DEL. ... we were afraid ...

DONNY. ... they didn't want it to Get Stolen.

JOHN. And the fishing line. Do we have that good line?

DEL. *(Simultaneous with "line.")* ... we were afraid it would get taken.

JOHN. ... that good heavy line...?

DONNY. ... I'm sorry, John...?

JOHN. The fishing line.

DONNY. I'm sure you. Yes. Fishing line. In the same box.

JOHN. Green? The green one?

DONNY. ... I ...

JOHN. The green line? In the Tackle Box? Because if not, we have to stop on the way, and ...

DONNY. ... I'm ...

JOHN. Dad said that the Green line ...

DEL. What's special about it?

DONNY. Open the box.

JOHN. ... because if not ...

DONNY. Find the box.

DEL. What's special about it?

JOHN. It's very strong.

DONNY. Find the box, open it, and check it out.

16

JOHN. Because that's how we'll know.

DONNY. That's what I'm telling you. *(John exits, up the stairs.)*

DEL. Port out, starboard home.

DONNY. And put some clothing on. *(Pause.)*

DEL. *(Of photo.)* ... when was this taken?

DONNY. I swear. He's ...

DEL. What? Well, he's having difficulty sleeping.

DONNY. It's all such a mystery.

DEL. Do you think?

DONNY. Yes. All our good intentions ...

DEL. Big thing. Going in the Woods. Your Father ...

DONNY. ... mmm.

DEL. ... big thing.

DONNY. Is it?

DEL. Hope to tell you.

DONNY. *(Pause.)* It goes so quickly.

DEL. Certain things remain.

DONNY. Yes?

DEL. *(Pause.) Friendship* ... *(Pause.)* Certain habits.

DONNY. It goes so quickly ... *(Pause.)*

DEL. Does it?

DONNY. Sometimes I wish I was a Monk.

DEL. Mmm ... what's that?

DONNY. I wish I were a monk.

DEL. How would that go?

DONNY. An old man for example ...

DEL. ... mmm ...

DONNY. *(Pause.)* ... and all his sons are gone.

DEL. ... an Oriental Fantasy.

DONNY. That's right.

DEL. "Mist".... "Mountains".... So on.

DONNY. ... mmm ...

DEL. And what does this man do?

DONNY. The monk.

DEL. Yes.

DONNY. Nothing. *(Pause.)* He sits; and gazes out at his ...

DEL. Mm. Well, that's a form of meditation ...

DONNY. Gazes out at his domain.

DEL.   Well, I'm sure you'd be very good at it.

DONNY.   You're very kind.

DEL.   What? I'm very kind, yes. *(Pause.)* For *it's*. A *form*. Of meditation. *(Pause.)* As are they all.

DONNY.   Mm.

DEL.   The thing about photography is that it is very seductive.

DONNY.   Because sometimes it seems the older I get, the less that I know.

DEL.   Well, it's a mystery. The whole goddamned thing.

DONNY.   Isn't it...?

DEL.   I think so. *(Pause.)* Goes fast. Goes quickly.

DONNY.   Mmm.

DEL.   ... and then it is gone. *(Pause.)*

DONNY.   No, I need a rest.

DEL.   *(Of photograph.)* Well, if we look here we see that the *tree* is gone. When would that have been?

DONNY.   *(To herself.)* A fantasy of rest ... *(Pause.)*

DEL.   ... Oh, oh, oh what are you doing this weekend...?

DONNY.   This weekend?

DEL.   Yes.

DONNY.   Well. I don't know.

DEL.   You don't know what you're doing this weekend.

DONNY.   I'm going to sit.

DEL.   To sit here.

DONNY.   Yes.

DEL.   Do you want company? *(John reenters, wrapped in a plaid blanket.)*

DONNY.   No. That's not clothing.

JOHN.   ... I ...

DONNY.   You put some clothing on right now. *(Pause.)* What? *(Pause.)*

JOHN.   I tore it.

DONNY.   You tore what?

JOHN.   I tore the blanket. I'm sorry.

DONNY.   You tore it?

JOHN.   *(Simultaneous with "tore.")* I was opening the box. I think there was a nail sticking out. I heard something rip ...

18

(He shows the tear.)

DONNY. You're saying you tore *that* blanket?

JOHN. I heard some …

DONNY. John …

JOHN. I was doing it too quickly. I know I heard.

DONNY. *(Simultaneous with "heard.")* John, that was torn so long ago.

JOHN. I heard it rip. *he becomes aware of the comfort being torn*

DONNY. No, it was torn years ago.

JOHN. *(Simultaneous with "ago.")* I didn't tear it?

DONNY. No.

JOHN. I heard it rip.

DEL. You may have heard it in your mind …

JOHN. … but …

DONNY. No we tore that long ago.

DEL. I think your mind is racing.

DONNY. It's all right, John. It's all right. Go upstairs. And you put on some clothing … *(Pause.)*

JOHN. It's tied with twine.

DONNY. I don't understand you.

JOHN. The *Tackle* box.

DONNY. Box …

JOHN. … with the fishing line …

DONNY. … well, *untie* it. And …

JOHN. I can't untie it. That's what I'm saying. I tried to pull the twine off, but …

DEL. *(Takes out knife. Of knife.)* This'll do it.

JOHN. I can't .

DEL. … is it all right …?

DONNY. … If you don't get some rest, before …

DEL. *(To Donny.)* Is it all right?

DONNY. What?

DEL. Can he have the knife?

DONNY. … to have the knife …

DEL. … to use. To cut the twine …

DONNY. *(Simultaneous with "twine.")* What would your father say?

JOHN. It's all right.

19

DONNY. He would?

JOHN. Yes.

DONNY. It's all right for you …

JOHN. … yes. Oh, yes.

DONNY. … to have the knife.

JOHN. Yes.

DONNY. *(Simultaneous with "Yes.")* I hardly think so.

JOHN. No he *would.*

DEL. Then there you go. *(Hands John the knife.)*

JOHN. Where did you get the knife, though?

DONNY. Good *Lord,* John … calm *down* tonight.

JOHN. No.

DONNY. What?

JOHN. I can't.

DONNY. … why not?

JOHN. The Tea, the Blanket…?

DONNY. I don't understand.

JOHN. I'm *waiting* for it.

DEL. You're waiting for what?

JOHN. "The Third Misfortune."

DEL. "The Third Misfortune."

DONNY. Third…?

JOHN. I'm waiting to see "What is the Third Misfortune?" *(Pause.)*

DONNY. What does he mean?

JOHN. It's in the book.

DEL. Misfortunes come in threes.

DONNY. Where *is* that book, by the way?

JOHN. Misfortunes come in threes.

DONNY. The third misfortune. I remember. Yes.

JOHN. It's in the book.

DONNY. Wait. How long since we've seen that book?

JOHN. A long time.

DONNY. Ha. And you remembered it?

JOHN. Of course I remember it.

DONNY. Isn't that odd?

JOHN. "When we think of sickness, sickness is approaching," said the Wizard.

DEL. ... That's what the Wizard said.

DONNY. Where *is* that book?

DEL. It will turn up someday.

DONNY. No, did we leave it at the lake?

JOHN. Misfortunes come in threes.

DONNY. All right, what are the three misfortunes?

JOHN. The Lance, and the Chalice; The Lance was broken by the Lord of Night, the Chalice was burnt ...

DONNY. Yes. No. Not in the book, here.

JOHN. What are the others here?

DONNY. The Three Misfortunes.

JOHN. *Here.*

DONNY. Yes.

JOHN. All right. One: The Pot, The Teapot broke.

DONNY. That's one, yes. And?

JOHN. The blanket.

DEL. ... the blanket.

DONNY. What about it?

JOHN. ... torn ...

DONNY. No, but it *wasn't* torn. That happened long ago.

JOHN. I *thought* I tore it now. *(Sound of teakettle, Donny exits.)*

DONNY. *(Offstage.)* It was torn long ago. You can absolve yourself.

JOHN. ... I *thought* that I tore it.

DEL. But, you see, in reality, things unfold ... independent of our fears of them.

JOHN. I don't know what you mean.

DEL. Because we *think* a thing is one way does not mean that this is the way that this thing must be.

JOHN. The blanket was torn long ago?

DEL. That's what your mother said.

JOHN. How?

DEL. Well ...

JOHN. Did you see my hat?

DEL. ... did?

JOHN. At the Cabin?

DEL. Which hat is that?

JOHN. The gray cap.

DEL. Like mine, except gray?

JOHN. Yes.

DEL. I don't remember.

JOHN. Not like yours, actually, it's ...

DEL. I don't remember.

JOHN. No, it's not actually like yours, it's . .

DEL. How is it different?

JOHN. It's. I steered you wrong. It's not like yours at all.

DEL. Then I don't know which one you mean.

JOHN. My *Gray* hat. It was on the peg.

DEL. The peg ...

JOHN. ... Near the door. At the cabin.

DEL. I don't remember.

JOHN. You don't? Why?

DEL. Because I wasn't looking for it. *(Pause.)* Do you know. I'm going to tell you a game.

JOHN. A game?

DEL. A game you can play. You and your father. Up there. Eh? To "sharpen your skills." *(Pause.)* To "aid your camping."

JOHN. Me and my father.

DEL. Yes.

JOHN. Does he know this game?

DEL. I think that he may.

JOHN. Did he teach it to you?

DEL. No. I learned it independently.

JOHN. Um.

DEL. And. If he does not know it, you can teach it to *him.*

JOHN. Good.

DEL. Yes? You think so?

JOHN. Well, I think so. You have to tell me the game.

DEL. Here it is: ... you write down ...

JOHN. "... to sharpen our skills ..."

DEL. You write down your *recollections*. Of the things you've seen. During the day. Then you compare them.

JOHN. I don't understand.

DEL. To see who has observed the best. You observe things during the day. Then, at night you write them down. To test your observation. *(Pause.)* Things in the Cabin, for instance.

Or the woods. And, then, you see whose recollection was more accurate. *(Pause.)* You see?

JOHN. See who was more accurate.

DEL. That's correct. *(Pause.)*

JOHN. And why is this game useful?

DEL. If you were lost it could assist you to orient yourself.

JOHN. Would it be things which we *decided before* to observe? Or things ...

DEL. ... it could be both.

JOHN. ... both things we *decided* to observe, and things we decided, later on, we should remember.

DEL. That's right.

JOHN. But something could have been the Third Misfortune, even though it had happened quite long ago. *(Pause.)*

DEL. How could that be?

JOHN. It could be if the "Third Misfortune" happened long ago. If, when it *happened,* no one *noticed,* or ...

DEL. "at the *time* ... "

JOHN. Yes, or neglected to *count* it ...

DEL. ... I ...

JOHN. ... until we recognized it *now.*... And also, what could we pick. To observe, beside the Cabin?

DEL. What? *Anything.* The *pond,* the ...

JOHN. ... where did you get the knife?

DEL. The knife.

JOHN. Yes.

DEL. I told you. Your father gave it to me.

JOHN. He gave you his war knife.

DEL. Yes.

JOHN. His *pilot's* knife...?

DEL. Yes. *(Pause.)*

JOHN. But we couldn't choose the pond.

DEL. Why not?

JOHN. Because it's changing. *(Pause.)* When?

DEL. ... when what?

JOHN. Did he give it to you?

DEL. Aha.

JOHN. When?

DEL.   Last week. When we went camping.

JOHN.   Oh.

DEL.   Does that upset you?

JOHN.   No.

DEL.   Aha.

JOHN.   What do you mean?

DEL.   Nothing.

JOHN.   Why did you say "aha."

DEL.   Something occurred to me.

JOHN.   What?

DEL.   Something. *(Pause.)*

JOHN.   We couldn't choose the pond.

DEL.   The pond?

JOHN.   To observe.

DEL.   No? Why not?

JOHN.   Because it's changing. *(Donny re-enters with tea mugs.)*

DEL.   Well, then you choose something else.

JOHN.   What should I choose?

DEL.   Something that doesn't change. *(Of photo.)* Who, who, what *is* this?

DONNY.   It's the Lake.

DEL.   No, please, I know where it is, I just don't ...

DONNY.   ... what?

DEL.   ... I don't remember it.

DONNY.   ... you've seen that photo so ...

DEL.   ... Well. I don't remember it.

JOHN.   You have a strange expression on your face. *Mother:* doesn't ...

DONNY.   Calm down. John.

DEL.   ... I do?

JOHN.   You're grinning. *(To Donny.)* I am calm.

DEL.   ... when was this taken? *(Donny looks at photo.)*

DONNY.   Well, the boathouse is still up ...

DEL.   *(To John.)* It's strange I'm grinning?

DONNY.   ... so it's ...

JOHN.   It looks unlike you.

DONNY.   *(Of photo, to Del.)* You don't remember this?

DEL.   No.

DONNY.   *Truly?*

DEL.   No. When was it taken?

DONNY.   *(Simultaneous with "taken.")* Well, all right: the boat-house is up, so, I can tell you what *year* it is: The boathouse is up, but the birch is down, so: it's before the War ...

DEL.   ... it would have to be before the War ...

DONNY.   *(Simultaneous with "war.")* Wait a moment ... *(John yawns. Sits on the couch.)* Oh, John; are you getting sleepy?

JOHN.   When is Dad coming home?

DONNY.   He'll be here when he gets here, I think.

JOHN.   ... I want to tell him this game.

DEL.   *(Of photograph.)* I remember the shirt.

DONNY.   ... he'll be home soon, John.

DEL.   ... is this Robert's shirt?   *← husband*

DONNY.   What?

DEL.   That I'm wearing.

DONNY.   In the photo ...

DEL.   Yes ...

DONNY.   ... I ... *(Pause.)*

DEL.   Do you see my problem? *(Pause.)*

DONNY.   All right.

DEL.   Because I remember neither the occasion nor the photograph.

DONNY.   ... Do you have his *shirt* on ...

DEL.   Yes.

DONNY.   Why *would* you?

DEL.   Well, that's what I'm saying.

DONNY.   Can you make the pattern out?

DEL.   He's asleep.

DONNY.   *Finally. (Pause.)* He thought that he tore the blanket.

DEL.   I believe that this Trip has a "meaning" for him.

DONNY.   Del, he's always had this problem.

DEL.   No, I've had a "clue."

DONNY.   No, you're ten years too late. You know, Robert always said: we disagreed about it. From the first. And his theory was "let the child cry."

DEL.   ... let him cry ...

DONNY.   To teach him to ...

DEL.   No, this trip ...

DONNY.   Del, He Always Has a Reason ...

DEL.   He's a sensitive kid...?

DONNY.   ... whatever that means.

DEL.   I think it means.... Well, in *this* case he *told* me, in effect.

DONNY.   ... yes?

DEL.   In *this* case it means he's *jealous.*

DONNY.   Jealous.

DEL.   Of my trip. Last week with Robert.

DONNY.   He was jealous?

DEL.   That's right.

DONNY.   But why does that come out *now?* And I'll tell you one other thing. *Let* him be jealous. What if he was? Yes. I think he needs to spend more time with his father; and, yes, I think that he has to learn the world does not revolve around him. *(Pause.)* Oh, Lord. I'll tell you. No. You're right. It's guilt. It's guilt. I'm guilty. I get to spend one weekend on my own. And I'm consumed with guilt.

DEL.   *(Of photo.)* Who took this picture? *(Pause. Donny looks at it.)*

DONNY.   I don't know.

DEL.   Eh? Who could have taken it?

DONNY.   Huh. *(Pause.)* I don't ...

DEL.   Do you see? If we're all in it? *(Pause.)* That's why I don't remember it.

DONNY.   I ... *(Pause.)* Isn't that funny...?

DEL.   That's why I don't remember it. *(Pause.)* I knew there was a reason. *(Pause.)*

DONNY.   Lord, I found so much *stuff* up there.

DEL.   ... up...?

DONNY.   In the attic. The *stadium* blanket, the ...

DEL.   I recognized that.

DONNY.   The blanket. Well I hope so.

DEL.   How could he think he tore it?

DONNY.   ... I ...

DEL.   He'd seen it for years.

DONNY. ... so long ago ...

DEL. Isn't it...? *(Pause.)* Do you know, at the Hotel. I collect things. I'm amazed. I clean my room out. Every few months. I'm amazed. I always think I've kept it *bare.* But when I clean it out. I find this mass of *things* I have accumulated.

DONNY. They, what are they, mostly?

DEL. Papers. *(Pause.)*

DONNY. I went to the Point.

DEL. You did?

DONNY. I walked down there. Yes.

DEL. Recently?

DONNY. Yes. *(Pause.)* And I remembered. When the Three of us would go. Late at night. Before the war.

DEL. I remember.

DONNY. And *Robert* and I. Would make love under a blanket. And I wondered. After all this time, why it never occurred to me. I don't know. But I wondered. Did you *hear* us; and, if you did. If it upset you. *(Pause.)*

DEL. And you've thought about it all this time.

DONNY. That's right.

DEL. Oh, Donny.

DONNY. Did it upset you?

DEL. Aren't you sweet ... aren't you sweet to worry.

DONNY. Did it?

DEL. Well. I ...

JOHN. *(Waking.)* What did they say? What?

DONNY. Go to sleep, John.

JOHN. I was going there. But you said to bring the, bring ... *(Pause.)* Bring them the ... *(Pause.)*

DONNY. John:

JOHN. ... huh ...

DONNY. It's all right.

JOHN. What did they talk about?

DONNY. John ...

JOHN. I don't like it. I don't like it. No.

DONNY. John ...

JOHN. I ... What? No. No. I don't want to. *(Pause.)* Is my father back yet?

27

DONNY. No. Why don't you go and get in bed ...

JOHN. When is he coming back?

DONNY. Very soon, I think.

JOHN. He is?

DONNY. Yes. Is that all right?

JOHN. *(Of photograph.)* You asked if the shirt you're wearing is his shirt.

DEL. What?

JOHN. ... in the photograph.

DEL. Is that His Shirt.

JOHN. You asked that.

DEL. Yes.

JOHN. Well, does it *look* like his shirt?

DEL. It's hard to tell. The picture is old ...

JOHN. *(To Donny.)* I didn't tear the blanket?

DONNY. No.

JOHN. You're certain.

DONNY. We've had it for years.

JOHN. I don't remember it.

DONNY. Yes. You would. If you thought about it.

JOHN. What was it?

DONNY. What? Go to sleep.

JOHN. What did you use it for?

DONNY. What did I use it for? A coverlet.

JOHN. To keep you warm.

DONNY. That's right.

JOHN. A coverlet.

DONNY. Yes.

JOHN. Where did it come from? The blanket.

DONNY. Where? In England.

JOHN. England.

DONNY. Yes. From an Arcade.

JOHN. Arcade ...

DONNY. With stores on either side.

JOHN. Did you buy it together?

DONNY. No. I bought it when he was away.

JOHN. Away.

DONNY. Yes. One day.

JOHN. Away in the War.

DONNY. That's right.. *(Pause.)*

JOHN. Did you miss him when he was gone?

DONNY. Yes, I did.

JOHN. What did you think about?

DONNY. *(Pause.)* Many things.

JOHN. What things did you think of?

DONNY. I don't know. *Many* things.

JOHN. Were you frightened for him?

DONNY. Yes. I was.

JOHN. Did you tell him?

DONNY. We used to go out. To the Country, you know …

JOHN. Is it wool …

DONNY. When he'd come back. Walk in a *field,* or …

JOHN. Is it wool?

DONNY. I'm sorry?

JOHN. Is it wool. The blanket.

DONNY. Do you know. When you were small. *You* slept in it. All of the time. We covered you.

JOHN. Why did you stop using it.

DONNY. We put it away.

JOHN. Why?

DONNY. It was torn. *(Pause.)* And now you go to sleep.

JOHN. Mother — Do you ever think you hear singing?

DONNY. I don't know what you mean.

JOHN. *Singing.*

DONNY. I don't know what you mean, John.

JOHN. At night. When you are asleep. Before you go to sleep.

DONNY. I don't know.

JOHN. … and you hear …

DONNY. … it's time for bed, now …

JOHN. … or you think you hear a *radio* …

DONNY. … a radio …

JOHN. Playing *music.* And you think. "Yes. I know. That's a radio." And you listen. But then, you say: "It's just in my head." But you can *listen* to it. It goes on. *(Pause.)* Or *voices.*

DONNY. You hear voices?

29

JOHN.   Just before you go to sleep. Do you ever do that? *(Pause.)* I <u>hear them. Outside my room.</u>
DONNY.   What are they saying?
JOHN.   Do you ever do that?
DONNY.   I don't know.
DEL.   What are your voices saying?
JOHN.   *(Simultaneous with "saying.")* Tell me how the blanket was torn.
DONNY.   You go to sleep now, John.
JOHN.   I want to see my father.
DONNY.   Yes. But now you go to sleep.
JOHN.   It's time to go to sleep.
DONNY.   That's right.
JOHN.   Is that right?
DONNY.   You have a big ...
JOHN.   *Tomorrow.*
DONNY.   Yes.
JOHN.   I'm going, you know, I'm going to do that thing.
DONNY.   What thing is that?
JOHN.   The Game.
DONNY.   ... the Game.
JOHN.   To remember. With him.
DONNY.   The game. Yes. *(John starts upstairs.)* You take the blanket.
JOHN.   To observe.
DONNY.   Mmm ...
JOHN.   ... but it would have to be some thing that would surprise us.
DONNY.   That's right.
JOHN.   When we look around. *(He continues up the stairs. Stops to lean over the landing. Looking down at the mantelpiece.)* So, I'll ask my Dad. First thing. "You tell me the name of an *object.*" Or a "*collection* of things" ... you know what I mean ...
DEL.   ... that's right.
JOHN.   "As we approach the Cabin."
DONNY.   Mm ...
JOHN.   "To test our skills."
DONNY.   ... mm.

JOHN. But it doesn't have to be the Cabin.

DEL. No ...

JOHN. It could be *anywhere* ...

DEL. That's right.

JOHN. It could be anywhere at all.

DEL. That's right. As long as it's some *thing*. You have determined to observe.

JOHN. Yes. I could be right here ...

DEL. That's absolutely right.

DONNY. *(Goes to him with the blanket. Simultaneous with "and.")* ... and take the blanket ...

DEL. Goodnight. John. *(John picks up white envelope.)*

DONNY. *(Of envelope.)* What have you got?

JOHN. Goodnight.

DONNY. ... what is that?

JOHN. It's a letter.... It's a note for you. *(She takes it, opens it.)* And it could be something right here, anything that, that, it would have to be something *new* ... something that would ...

DONNY. ... that's right ...

JOHN. ... *surprise* us.

DONNY. ... when did this get here...?

JOHN. ... you see?

DONNY. John. Got to bed. Now. Yes.

JOHN. Do you see?

DONNY. Go to bed.

JOHN. All right. I understand. I'm going.

DEL. Goodnight, John. *(John exits.)* What is it?

DONNY. It's a letter to me. *(Pause.)*

DEL. A letter. *(Pause.)* What does it say?

DONNY. My husband's leaving me.

DEL. He's leaving you. *(Pause.)* Why would he want to that...?

END OF ACT ONE

31

ACT TWO

The next night.

John, in his bathrobe, and Donny.

JOHN.   I thought that maybe there was nothing there. *(Pause.)* I thought that nothing was *there.* Then I was looking at my *book.* I thought "Maybe there's nothing *in* my book." It talked about the *buildings.* Maybe there's nothing *in* the buildings. And ... or on *my globe.* You know my globe? You know my globe?

DONNY.   Yes.

JOHN.   Maybe there's nothing on the thing that it is of. We don't know what's there. *We* don't know that those things are there.

DONNY.   I've been there. To many of them.

JOHN.   Or in *buildings* we have not been in. Or in *history.* In the *history* of things. Or *thought. (Pause.)* I was *lying* there, and maybe there is no such thing as *thought.* Who *says* there is? Or human beings. And we are a dream. Who knows we are here? No one knows we are. We are a dream. We are just *dreaming.* I *know* we are. Or else ... or else ... *(Pause.)* ... and how do we *know* the things we know? We don't know what's real. And all we do is *say* things. *(Pause.)* Where do we *get* them from? And, or that things, go on forever. *(Pause.)* Or that we're *born.* Or that dead people moan. Or that, or that there's *hell.* And maybe we are there. Maybe there are people who've *been* there. Or, or else why should we *think* it? That's what I don't know. And maybe *everything* is true. Maybe it's true that I'm *sitting* here ...

DONNY.   Johnnie.

JOHN.   What...?

DONNY.   I think ...

JOHN.   ... don't you think?

DONNY. ... you have to ...

JOHN. No, I don't.

DONNY. Please, please do, though.

JOHN. I don't want to, though. *(Del enters. Of Del.)* That's what I mean. I don't want to ... didn't you, mother. Mother ...

DONNY. *(To Del.)* Did you ...

DEL. *(Simultaneous with you.)* No.

DONNY. Did you find him?

DEL. *(To John.)* How are you? *(To Donny.)* No.

JOHN. I'm fine.

DONNY. Where did you look?

DEL. The *Windemere,* and then I stopped at Jimmy's.

DONNY. Did you try The Eagle?

DEL. No. *(Unpacking his paper bag.)* How has he ...

DONNY. Why *not?* Why *not?*

DEL. I'm sorry ... why not what?

DONNY. *(Simultaneous with "what.")* Why didn't you go to the ...

DEL. ... I thought you were going to call them.

DONNY. Why should I call them, if they'll say he wasn't *there?* Even if he *is* there...?

DEL. *(Simultaneous with "there.")* I thought you were going to call them.

DONNY. *(Simultaneous with "call.")* No. I never said that.

DEL. Well, then, I made a mistake. *(He is preparing syrup from medicine bottle.)*

DONNY. How much was it?

DEL. I told them to charge it to you. *(Holding spoon. To John.)* Open your mouth.

JOHN. I don't want to take that stuff.

DONNY. You're going to take it and you're going to *sleep.*

JOHN. No. I'm not sleepy.

DONNY. Take the medicine. Did you *hear* me? You're *sick,* and you're going to *bed.*

JOHN. I can't *sleep.*

DEL. ... that's why ...

JOHN. Every time I go to sleep I *see* things ...

DONNY. You must ...

DEL.   That's, that's why you have to take the medicine, John.

JOHN.   *(Simultaneous with "John.")* No. I'm not tired.

DONNY.   Do you want to go to the Hospital?

JOHN.   No.

DONNY.   No? Did you hear what The Doctor said?

JOHN.   No.

DEL.   ... what did he say?

DONNY.   I want you to go to bed *now.*

DEL.   You heard your mother.

JOHN.   No. No.

DONNY.   Johnnie ...

JOHN.   No one understands. You think that I'm *in* something.... You don't know what I'm feeling.

DEL.   What are you feeling? *(Pause.)* Are you afraid to go to bed?

JOHN.   Yes.

DONNY.   Why?

DEL.   What are you afraid of in there?

JOHN.   I don't know.

DONNY.   I ... I ... I know it *frightens* you ...

JOHN.   I don't want to go to sleep.

DEL.   All right, all right, I'm going to *promise* you ... look at me. John. I'm going to *promise* you if you take this and ... you take this and go upstairs then you won't be afraid. I promise. *(Pause.)* I promise you. *(Pause.)*

JOHN.   I sweat through the sheets ...

DEL.   We'll change ...

JOHN.   ... the *bed* is wet.

DEL.   We'll change, we'll change the sheets, you don't have to worry.

DONNY.   You go lie down in my bed.

DEL.   ... you lie down in your mother's bed. *(Pause.)* You go lie down there.

JOHN.   I'm going to sweat them.

DEL.   That's all right. Do you hear what I'm telling you...? *(Pause.)*

JOHN.   Maybe I'll just ... maybe I'll just go there ... maybe I'll just go there and lie down.

34

DONNY.   Yes. You go and lie down now. You take this, now. *(Del gives John his medicine.)*

JOHN.   Do you know why I took it, 'cause I'm tired.

DEL.   I'm sure you are.

JOHN.   ... 'cause I've been *up* all day ...

DEL.   I know you have. And I know how that feels.

JOHN.   I ... I ...

DONNY.   ... you go to bed now.

DEL.   John? "My blessing on this house...," the Wizard said.

JOHN.   When is my father coming for me...?

DONNY.   Shhhh.

JOHN.   ... No. I don't understand.

DONNY.   Shh. It's all right.

JOHN.   What's happening to me...?

DONNY.   *(Embracing him.)* It's all right. Hush. You go to bed. It's all right. John. Shh. You've only got a fever. Shhh ...

DEL.   ... you're fine ...

DONNY.   You go upstairs now. Shhh. You go upstairs now, John ... *(She starts him upstairs. Comes down.)*

DEL.   ... I looked every place I thought that he would *be* ...

DONNY.   I'm sorry.

DEL.   But I couldn't find him. *(Pause.)* Do you want a drink?

DONNY.   No. *(Pause.)*

DEL.   I'm sorry that I couldn't find him. *(Pause.)* Would you like me to go out again?

DONNY.   No. *(Pause.)*

DEL.   Would you like to play Casino?

DONNY.   No.

DEL.   No, you're right, that's stupid. Oh God, oh God, that's *stupid. (Pause.)* Would you like to play Gin?

DONNY.   Del ...

DEL.   Yeah. Do you see what I mean when I talk about myself? *(Pause.)* But would you like to?

DONNY.   Let's have a drink.

DEL.   Well. I know I know I'm limited. *(Del goes to the liquor cabinet, examines bottles.)* There's only a new one.

DONNY.   That's all right, open it. Enough. Enough for one day. I don't care. *(Pause.)* I don't care anymore. I swear to

God. *(Del takes out bottle, takes out his knife, opens it.)*

DEL. *(Of bottle.)* I think that this is good for you. *(Pause.)* You know why...? Because it's a ceremony. To, to *delimit* umm

DONNY. A ceremony.

DEL. Of ... of what? Of, of *inebriation,* certainly, of, of of well, of *togetherness* ... I don't know. *(He goes to the kitchen, comes out with two glasses and the bottle. Pours two glasses.)*

DONNY. Thank you.

DEL. Uh ... Days May Come and Days May Go *(Pause.)* Well, *that's* true enough.

DONNY. Isn't it?

DEL. I think so. *(Pause.)* Days May Come and Go.

DONNY. And May we Always be as ...

DEL. Yes.

DONNY. As ...

DEL. Unified.

DONNY. Well, let's pick something more moving than that.

DEL. All right ... be. be. be. be-*nighted?* No, that's not the word I want to use ... be-*trothed...?* No.

DONNY. Close ...

DEL. Yes.

DONNY. Close to each other.

DEL. As we happen to be right now. *(Pause.)*

DONNY. Fine.

DEL. *(Pause.)* And ... May the Spirit of Friendship ... *(Pause.)* oh, the hell with it. I mean, can't people just have a drink ... for the love of God? *(They drink.)* Bec, because I swear, because I think there's just too much. In *trial* ... in *adversity* ... *(Pause.)* and you can't, you can't go always look ...

DONNY. Go Looking for *answers.*

DEL. No.

DONNY. ... you're absolutely right ...

DEL. In intro*spec*tion *(Pause.)* You know, at times of *trial* ...

DONNY. hmm ...

DEL. Do you hear what I'm telling you?

DONNY. Yes.

DEL. ... and they come for us all.

DONNY. ... Oh, Lord.

DEL. Yes. They do. Then many times the answer comes. In reaching out. Or, do you know what? In getting drunk.

DONNY. ... in drinking.

DEL. Be. Because, you know? Then you forget. *(Pause.)* And I don't *give* a damn. *(Pause.)* In this *shithole.* *(Pause.)* Well. I'm not going to *dwell* upon it. *(Pause.)* You drink, and then, when you *remember* again—this is the good part—when you *remember* again ... *(Pause.)* It's later on. And time has dulled your, your ... you know, for whatever portion of time that, that you for-*got.* *(Pause.)*

DONNY. "You should get married."

DEL. "It would have to be someone nice."

DONNY. "We'll find them for you."

DEL. "Would you?" *(Pause.)* Although we joke about it. *(Sighs.)* Do you want me to go and look at John?

DONNY. He's going to be all right.

DEL. Are *you* all right, though?

DONNY. Yes.

DEL. I'm sorry that I didn't find Robert.

DONNY. *(Simultaneous with "find.")* ...That's

DEL. I *looked* for him, but ...

DONNY. That's al ...

DEL. I didn't find him. I suppose I thought that — in, you know, in addition to the things I said — that it wasn't a good *idea* to have him come here. But what business is that if *mine?* *(Pause.)* None. None, really.

DONNY. That's all right.

DEL. None at all. But I *looked* for him. *(Pause.)*

DONNY. *(Long pause.)* Well ...

DEL. Worse things have happened, I suppose. *(Pause.)*

DONNY. ... mmm.

DEL. It's such a shock.

DONNY. However much we ...

DEL. What?

DONNY. I'm sorry?

DEL. However much...?

DONNY. We could have anticipated it.

DEL. How could we?

DONNY. He tried to tell you.

DEL. What do you mean?

DONNY. He gave you the knife.

DEL. I don't understand.

DONNY. The Odd Gesture. *(Pause.)* Isn't it.

DEL. I don't understand.

DONNY. You don't understand the Gesture?

DEL. No.

DONNY. It was his going-away present. *(Pause.)* Going away. *(Pause.)* Big German knife. His war memento. Do you know the Meaning of it?

DEL. ... meaning ...

DONNY. You know what it's for.

DEL. The knife.

DONNY. Yes.

DEL. *(Pause.)* To cut things.

DONNY. I mean the specific ...

DEL. The specific *purpose?* No. No. I mean, *no.*

DONNY. It's a *pilot's* knife ...

DEL. ... yes. I know that ...

DONNY. If he was forced to *parachute* ...

DEL. Yes.

DONNY. The pilot would use it to cut the *cords.* If his parachute snagged.

DEL. Huh. If it snagged. On, on what?

DONNY. On a tree.

DEL. Oh, you mean when he landed.

DONNY. Yes.

DEL. Huh. *(Pause.)*

DONNY. And that's the meaning. *(Pause.)*

DEL. ... yes ...

DONNY. When he was forced to abandon ...

DEL. Yes. *(Pause.)* When he was forced to *abandon* his ... *(Pause.)* He looked for *safety,* and the knife, it cut.... It "released" him.

DONNY. Yes. That's right.

DEL. ... as *any* tool ...

DONNY. And he gave it to you.

DEL. He can be very generous. Is that all right? To …

DONNY. Yes. No. He can. *(Pause.)* … what am I going to do? You tell me. Yes. He could be generous. *I* don't know.

DEL. … he was opening a can. With it. And I said … actually, he saw me looking at the knife. And he wiped it. And gave it to me. *(Pause.)*

DONNY. When you were at the Camp. Last week.

DEL. That's right — *(Pause.)*

DONNY. Tell me what you talked about.

DEL. What we talked about. In the Woods.

DONNY. Yes.

DEL. We talked about you.

DONNY. About *me…?*

DEL. Yes. *(Pause.)*

DONNY. What did he say?

DEL. How happy he had been.

DONNY. Really.

DEL. That's what he said.

DONNY. How can you understand that. *(Pause.)* How in the world …

DEL. I'm so sorry.

DONNY. Did you know he was leaving me?

DEL. No.

DONNY. Did you think that he was?

DEL. No.

DONNY. No? You didn't?

DEL. How could I?

DONNY. … he didn't…?

DEL. No. He didn't what…?

DONNY. Give you a sign…?

DEL. A sign. No.

DONNY. How can we understand … how … *men*, you know. How … men …

DEL. I'm going to *tell* you something. It's funny for two grown men to go camping anyway. *(Pause.)* I don't care. *(Pause.)* Huh. I was born a *city* boy. *(Pause. He displays knife.)* And now I'm a Forester. *(Pause.)* I'm a Ranger … did you know there's a Fraternal Group called the Catholic Order of

39

Foresters?

DONNY. Yes.

DEL. You knew that?

DONNY. Yes. Sure.

DEL. I wonder what they do. *(Pause.)*

DONNY. Did you say he gave that knife to you when you went camping?

DEL. Yes. *(Pause.)*

DONNY. When the two of you went camping. Last ...

DEL. Last week. That's right. *(Pause.)*

DONNY. He gave the knife to you.

DEL. Yes. He was opening a can of ... *(Pause.)* Why? *(Pause.)* Why did you ask?

DONNY. I saw it in the attic. When I went up there. To put the things away.

DEL. *(Pause.)* What things?

DONNY. When I took the camping things up. Last week. *(Pause.)* After your trip. When you came back.

DEL. I don't understand.

DONNY. When you came back, last week, Robert and you.

DEL. ... yes ...

DONNY. From your Trip. I went up. To put his things away. And the knife was up there. *(Pause.)* It was already in the attic.

DEL. Well, maybe he went up there first, to put it back.

DONNY. ... What?

DEL. I'm saying, maybe Robert went there first to put it back. When we came back. When we came back from *camping.* *(Pause.)* I'm sure that's what occurred. *(Pause.)*

DONNY. You're saying that he went upstairs to put it back.

DEL. Yes. Because it was precious to him.

DONNY. I don't understand.

DEL. It was a *war* memento. I'm saying that it was so *precious* to him that he went, and *left* the stuff ... for *you* to put away, but went upstairs and put the *knife* into the trunk himself. *(Pause.)*

DONNY. Then how did *you* get it? *(Pause.)*

DEL. What?

DONNY. How did you get the knife?

DEL. He gave it to me.

DONNY. I don't understand.

DEL. He gave it to me.

DONNY. How could he give it to you?

DEL. What?

DONNY. You said he gave it to you when you were camping. *(Pause.)* How could he give it to you when you were *camping*, when it was here in the trunk when you both came back? *(Pause.)*

DEL. There must be two knives. *(Pause.)*

DONNY. I ... I don't understand.

DEL. There must be two knives.

DONNY. What?

DEL. I bet if you went in the trunk to look right now you'd see. There was another knife.

DONNY. Yes. No. Wait.... When did Robert give the knife to you?

DEL. I *thought* ... isn't it funny? I was sure he gave the knife to me while we were camping. I guess I'm mistaken. *(Pause.)* Huh. *(Pause.)* Unless, no.... Huh!... I ... I don't know. *(Pause.)* It's a mystery to me. Unless ...

DONNY. *Wait!*

DEL. What?

DONNY. He came upstairs. He came up. To the attic!

DEL. Who?

DONNY. I was putting the things away. He said. Yes. "Leave the trunk open." *(Pause.)* He *got* it from the trunk. When you came back. He didn't *put* it there. He went up there to *get* it. *(Pause.)*

DEL. That could happen.

DONNY. What do you mean?

DEL. Well, that, that's not so unusual.

DONNY. What isn't.

DEL. ... for someone to do that. *(Pause.)*

DONNY. Did he do that?

DEL. It's possible. I think he did. Yes. I think *that's*. Um that's *exactly* what he did. I *think*. *(Pause.)*

DONNY. Why did you lie to me?

DEL. I didn't lie. It was a slip of memory.

DONNY. Why did you lie?

DEL. If I did I *assure* you, it was, um, *you* know ...

DONNY. What?

DEL. It was ...

DONNY. You didn't go camping.

DEL. Who?

DONNY. You and Robert.

DEL. That's ridiculous!

DONNY. You never went.

DEL. That's ...

DONNY. ... Yes...?

DEL. Be, because, be ... what are you *saying* to me? Am, am I to be *accused* of this!

DONNY. Of what?

DEL. Well, that's my point.

DONNY. What did you do?

DEL. I. Why do you say *that*? For god*sake!*

DONNY. What did you do? I'll ask Robert.

DEL. You can't find him!

DONNY. What do you mean?

DEL. He won't tell you. *(Pause.)* All right. *(Pause.)* But: I want to *tell* you something: I knew that I should not take that knife.

DONNY. Why did you take it?

DEL. Be, because he *gave* it to me.

DONNY. Why? *(Pause.)*

DEL. Huh. Well, that's the *question. (Pause.) That's* what you'd like to *know. (Pause.) Isn't* it? Yes. So you could say, "Old Del, who we thought was so Loyal" ... I know what you mean. Be*lieve* me. *(Pause.)* Believe me.

DONNY. Why did he give the knife to you?

DEL. You don't want to know.

DONNY. I do.

DEL. *Believe* me, you don't. *(Pause.)* To shut me up. All right? There. Are you *happy?* I told you you wouldn't be.

DONNY. To shut you up about what? *(Pause.)*

DEL. Because we didn't go.

DONNY. What?

DEL. We didn't *go!* Do I have to *shout* it for you...? We stayed *home*. What do you *think?* He'd traipse off in the *wilds* ... with *me...?* To talk about *life?* Are you *stupid?* Are you *blind?* He wouldn't spend a *moment* with me. Some poor geek ... "Here's my Old Friend Del ..." You're *nuts,* you're *stupid* if you think that's what went on. *(Pause.)* He used my *room,* all right? He said, "Del, can I Use Your Room?" Is that so weird? There. Now I've told you. Now you can sleep easier. *I told* you not to ask. Don't tell me I didn't tell you. *(Pause.)*

DONNY. He used your room.

DEL. That's absolutely right.

DONNY. Why? *(Pause.)*

DEL. To go there with a woman. *(Pause.)* And now, and now you know the truth, How weak I arm. How "Evil" I am. He said, "I have some things to do," "I want it to seem like I'm gone." *I* spent the week, *I* slept in the, in my, my nook in the *library*. In *fishing* clothes ... and don't you think *that* looked stupid! *(Pause.)* I ... I, actually, I've been waiting for this. I knew that I should tell you. This is the only bad thing I have ever done to you. I'm sorry that it came out like this. Indeed I am. *(Pause.)* But we can't always choose the, um ... *(Pause.)*

DONNY. Get out. *(Pause.)* Get out. *(Del exits. Pause. Donny starts to cry. Pause.)* Bobby. Bobby. Bobby. *(John appears in bathrobe. Pause.)*

JOHN. Are you dead?

DONNY. What?

JOHN. Are you dead? *(Pause.)*

DONNY. Why do you say that?

JOHN. *(Simultaneous with "that.")* I heard you calling.

DONNY. Go back to bed, John.

JOHN. I heard voices ...

DONNY. ... you should go back to bed.

JOHN. ... and I thought they were you. *(Pause.)*

DONNY. It was me.

JOHN. And so I said, "... there's someone troubled." And I walked around. Did you hear walking?

DONNY. No.

JOHN. ... and so I went outside. I saw a candle. In the dark.

DONNY. Where was this?

JOHN. In my room. It was burning there. I said, "I'm perfectly alone." This is what I was saying to myself: "I'm perfectly alone." And I think I was saying it a long time. 'Cause I didn't have a pen. Did that ever happen to you?

DONNY. I don't know, John.

JOHN. So I came downstairs to write it down. I know that there *are* pens up there. But I don't want to look for them. *(Donny goes to him and cradles him.)* Do you think that was right?

DONNY. Shhh.

JOHN. Do you think that I was right?

DONNY. Go to bed.

JOHN. Mother? *(Pause.)*

DONNY. What?

JOHN. Do you think that I was right.

DONNY. I don't know, John.

JOHN. I saw a candle in my room.

END OF ACT TWO

44

ACT THREE

Evening. One month later.

The room is denuded. Various packing boxes are seen. John is sitting on one of them. Donny comes downstairs carrying a box. She puts it down and starts for the kitchen.

JOHN.   Where were you?

DONNY.   I'll put the kettle on.

JOHN.   *(Simultaneous with "on.")* Where were you?

DONNY.   I went up for your bag.

JOHN.   The movers will take it.

DONNY.   There were some things I thought that you might like to have.

JOHN.   What things?

DONNY.   For the first few nights. *(Pause.)* Until the boxes come. *(She starts into the kitchen.)*

JOHN.   Mother.

DONNY.   *(Offstage.)* … yes …

JOHN.   Do you ever think things? *(Pause.)* Mother…?

DONNY.   *(Offstage, simultaneous with "mother.")* What? *(Pause.)* What, John? *(Donny re-enters.)* What did you say?

JOHN.   I asked you. Do you think things.

DONNY.   What things, John? *(Pause.)*

JOHN.   Do you ever wish that you could die? *(Pause.)*

DONNY.   … do I wish I could die?

JOHN.   Yes. *(Pause.)*

DONNY.   I don't know.

JOHN.   Yes, you do.

DONNY.   No, I don't know, John.

JOHN.   Yes you do. You can tell me. *(Pause.)* It's not such a bad feeling. *(Pause.)* Is it?

DONNY.   I don't know.

JOHN.   Yes. You do. *(Pause.)* I think you do.

DONNY.   John: Things occur. In our lives. And the mean-

45

ing of them ... the *meaning* of them ... is not clear.

JOHN.   ... the meaning of them ...

DONNY.   That's correct. At the time. But we assume they have a meaning. We must. And we don't know what it is.

JOHN.   Do you ever wish you could die? *(Pause.)* Would you tell me?

DONNY.   Do I wish that I could die?

JOHN.   You can tell me. You won't frighten me.

DONNY.   *(Pause.)* How can I *help* you? Do you see? *(Pause.)* Do you see?

JOHN.   No.

DONNY.   At some point ... there are things that have occurred I cannot help you with ... that ...

JOHN.   I can't sleep.

DONNY.   Well. It's an unsettling time.

JOHN.   ... I want ...

DONNY.   Yes?

JOHN.   I would like to go to the Cabin.

DONNY.   ... well ...

JOHN.   I want to go to the Lake.

DONNY.   Well, no, John, we can't. You know we can't.

JOHN.   I don't know that.

DONNY.   No. We can't.

JOHN.   That's why I can't sleep.

DONNY.   What do you want me to do? John? I am not God. I don't control the World. If you could think what it is I could do for you.... If I could help you ... *(Sound of kettle, offstage.)*

JOHN.   Do you ever wish you could die? *(Pause.)* It's not such a bad feeling. Is it?

DONNY.   I know that you're frightened. I know you are. But at some point, do you see...? *(Pause. Exits. Offstage.)* John, everyone has a story. Did you know that? In their lives. This is yours. *(Del enters.)* And finally ... finally ... you are going to have to learn how you will deal with it. You understand? I'm going to speak to you as an adult. At some point.... At some point, we have to learn to face ourselves ... what kind of tea ...

46

DEL.   Hello.

JOHN.   Hello.

DEL.   How are you today?

JOHN.   I'm fine.

DONNY.   *(Offstage.)* What kind of tea?

DEL.   That's good.

DONNY.   *(Offstage.)* John?

JOHN.   What did my mother say?

DEL.   I came to talk to you.

JOHN.   *(Simultaneous with "you.")* ... what did my mother say?

DEL.   *(Simultaneous with "say.")* She wanted to know what kind of tea ...

DONNY.   *(Offstage.)* John...?

DEL.   ... what sort of tea you wanted. What sort of tea *do* you want? *(John rises to exit.)*

JOHN.   I don't know.

DEL.   I'd like to talk to you, John.

JOHN.   About what?

DEL.   Several things.

JOHN.   When is my father coming?

DEL.   I have something that I'd like to say.

JOHN.   I have to go upstairs.

DEL.   Could you wait a moment? *(John exits.)* John ...

DONNY.   *(Offstage.)* Do you see? One has to go on. That's all we can say. I'm speaking to you as an adult. *(She enters, with a tea tray. Pause.)* Where's my son?

DEL.   I don't know. He went upstairs. *(Pause.)*

DONNY.   Mm.

DEL.   That's right.

DONNY.   How is my husband.

DEL.   I don't see him.

DONNY.   No...?

DEL.   I came to talk to you. And to the boy.

DONNY.   Well, it seems that he's gone upstairs.

DEL.   Aha.

DONNY.   What do you need to say? *(Pause.)*

DEL.   I'm sorry what I did. *(Pause.)* Aren't we a funny race? The things we do. *(Pause.)* And then what we say about them.

You'd think, if there were a "Deity" we would all burn. *(Pause.)* Swine that we are. But we go on. *(Pause.)* I brought something for you.

DONNY.　You did?

DEL.　*(Produces book.)* As you see.

DONNY.　And that's supposed to put you back in my good graces?

DEL.　What would do that?

DONNY.　Nothing you've brought.

DEL.　Well. *(Pause.)* Here is a book. It's your book, by the way. I've kept it. All these years. Perhaps that's what rooted my soul. Do you know, they say: it is not the sins we commit that destroy us, but how we act after we've committed them. Is that a useful bit of lore? *(Pause.)* I've found it so. *(Pause.)* And here is the German Pilot's Knife. I was obsessed to bring it. I thought, "But why would she want it?" But, of course, it's not for you. It's a propitiation. To the boy.

DONNY.　To the boy ...

DEL.　Yes. Well, he should have it. Shouldn't he?

DONNY.　Should he?

DEL.　Yes.

DONNY.　Why?

DEL.　Because I've wronged him.

DONNY.　You've wronged him.

DEL.　I have.

DONNY.　Haven't you wronged me?

DEL.　What was I going to bring you, Flowers?

DONNY.　But you brought the boy the knife.

DEL.　That's right.

DONNY.　No, you puzzle me.

DEL.　*I* don't deserve it. It's his father's, um, what do they call it? "War" memento. A "combat" trophy. I brought you the bbb ...

DONNY.　... it's not a "combat" ...

DEL.　I brought you the *book* ...

DONNY.　It's not a combat trophy.

DEL.　Well, well, it's a *War* memen ...

DONNY.　It's not a Combat Trophy.

DEL.   *Whatever* it is.

DONNY.   It's not ...

DEL.   All right. He won it in the War. I didn't want to deprive the boy of ...

DONNY.   He didn't win it in the war.

DEL.   *Really.*

DONNY.   No.

DEL.   No. The German Knife.

DONNY.   No.

DEL.   Well, of *course* he did.

DONNY.   Not in the "fighting."

DEL.   Oh. He didn't...?

DONNY.   No. Not in the "fighting." No.

DEL.   He didn't get it in the fighting.

DONNY.   No.

DEL.   Well, yes, he did.

DONNY.   How could he?

DEL.   Well, you tell me. How could he *not?* It's a *war* mem ...

DONNY.   He was a flier. Do you see?

DEL.   No.

DONNY.   He was a flier.

DEL.   I don't see.

DONNY.   He was in the *air.* Could he capture the knife in the Air?

DEL.   I don't understand.

DONNY.   Could he get it in the Air? You "fairy"? Could he capture the knife from the other man in the Air? You fool.

DEL.   *(Pause.)* Then how did he obtain it?

DONNY.   How do you think?

DEL.   I don't know.

DONNY.   But how do you think?

DEL.   I don't know. That's why I ask.

DONNY.   He bought it.

DEL.   He bought the knife.

DONNY.   That's right.

DEL.   The Combat knife.

DONNY.   Mm.

49

DEL.   ... he gave me.

DONNY.   Yes.

DEL.   Where?

DONNY.   From a man. On the street. In London.

DEL.   Huh. *(Pause.)* You're saying he bought the knife. And you thought that would hurt me. *(Pause.)* And you're right of course.

DONNY.   ... to hurt you.

DEL.   Well, you knew it would.

DONNY.   Why would that hurt you?

DEL.   Oh, you didn't know that.

DONNY.   No.

DEL.   Then why did you say it?

DONNY.   I ...

DEL.   Why did you say it, then? Excuse me, that the souvenir that he gave me, as a War Memento, with "associations," that it had no meaning for him. And what would *I* know about the war? I live in a *Hotel. (Pause.)*

DONNY.   I didn't mean to hurt you.

DEL.   Oh, if we could speak the truth, do you see, for one instant. Then we would be free. *(Pause.)* I should have chucked it anyway. *(Pause.)* How could a knife be a suitable gift for a child? No, but we know it can't. We bring our ... our little "gifts." And take your book. It's your goddamn book. I've had it at the hotel. All these years. I borrowed it and never brought it back. How about that. Eh? Years ago. That's how long I've had it. Was ever anyone so false? Take it. I hate it. I hate the whole fucking progression. Here. Take the cursed thing. *(Hands her the book.)*

DONNY.   It's your copy.

DEL.   It is?

DONNY.   Yes.

DEL.   How do you know?

DONNY.   It's got your name in it. *(Pause.)*

DEL.   Where? *(She shows him. Of book.)* This *is* my copy ... isn't that funny? *(Pause.)* Because I'd *wondered* what I'd done with it. Do you know how long I've been *looking* for this? *(Pause. Reads.)* "May you always be as ..."

DONNY.   Aren't you funny.

DEL.   I'm pathetic. I know that. You don't have to tell me. The life that I lead is trash. I hate myself. Oh well. *(Pause.)* But I would like to talk to you. *(Pause.)* If I might. *(Pause.)* In spite of ...

DONNY.   In spite of ...

DEL.   What has occurred. *(Pause.)*

DONNY.   Why?

DEL.   Because there are things. I have been longing to say. To, um ... "say," for a long.... And perhaps this is what it takes. Isn't it funny? If you'd permit me. All right. Thank you. For a long while ... *(John appears on the stairs.)*

DONNY.   *(Pause.)* Yes? Yes, John...?

JOHN.   I'm cold. I'm sorry. *(Pause.)* I'm cold. My *mind* is racing. I ...

DONNY.   You what? *(Pause.)*

JOHN.   ... I think ...

DONNY.   ... what can I do about it?

JOHN.   I ...

DONNY.   What can I *do* about it, John?

JOHN.   I don't know.

DONNY.   What do you expect me to do?

JOHN.   I don't know.

DONNY.   Well.

DEL.   ... may I speak to him?

JOHN.   I don't, I'm afraid. I know that I should not *think* about certain things, but ...

DEL.   *(To Donny.)* May...?

JOHN.   ... but I ...

DONNY.   John: John: I'd like to help you; now: you have to go to sleep. You must go to sleep. If you do *not* sleep, *lay* there. Lay in bed. What you think about there is your concern. No one can help you . Do you understand? *Finally, each of us.* ⟶ desolation

JOHN.   Where is the blanket?

DONNY.   I.... *Each* of us ...

JOHN.   I want the blanket.

DONNY.   Is alone.

51

JOHN. ... the *stadium* blanket.
DONNY. *(Simultaneous with "stadium.")* I've put it away.
JOHN. No: Mother ...
DEL. May I speak to him?
JOHN. I want it.
DONNY. I've put it away, John
JOHN. I'm cold. Could I have it, please.
DONNY. It's packed away.
JOHN. Where?
DONNY. A box. Up in the attic, I believe ...
DEL. *(Simultaneous with "believe.")* It's in the attic, John.
JOHN. I need it. I'm cold.
DONNY. John.... All right, now.
JOHN. ...
DEL. *(To Donny.)* Perhaps he ...
DONNY. It's packed in a box.
DEL. But couldn't he get it, though?
DONNY. No. It's waiting for the *movers.*
DEL. But might he have it?
DONNY. It's wrapped up.
JOHN. I could undo it.
DONNY. Fine. Then it's in the attic. In the large brown box.
DEL. You see?
JOHN. Yes.
DONNY. With the new address on it.
JOHN. And I can open it. The box?
DONNY. If you will go to sleep. You must go to sleep. Do you hear me?
DEL. That is the point, do you see? John?
DONNY. You can unwrap it if you go to sleep.
DEL. ... that's right.
DONNY. But you must ...
DEL. We're talking to you like a man.
DONNY. But you must promise ...
JOHN. ... I promise.
DONNY. ... Because ...
JOHN. I understand. I promise. *(Pause.)* I promise.
DONNY. Do you understand?

JOHN.   Yes. Yes. I promise.

DEL.   Good, then, John. Goodnight.

DONNY.   Goodnight. *(John exits. Pause.)* Lucky boy. To have a protector. *(Pause.)*

DEL.   Well ...

DONNY.   Don't you think?

DEL.   Donny, I ...

DONNY.   Do you know. If I could find one man in my life. Who would not betray me. *(Pause.)*

DEL.   I'm sorry.

DONNY.   That's what I mean.

DEL.   I'm sorry I betrayed you.

DONNY.   Isn't that sweet. Aren't you sweet. How could one be miffed with you? The problem must be *mine*.

DEL.   I'm sorry I betrayed you.

DONNY.   Just like the rest of them. All of you are.

DEL.   I'm sorry.

DONNY.   Can you explain it to me, though? Why? *(Pause.)* You see? That's what baffles me. I try to say "human nature" ...

DEL.   ... I know ...

DONNY.   I don't know what our nature is. If I do, then it's bad.

DEL.   ... I know ...

DONNY.   If I do, then it's filthy. No, you don't know. You have no idea. All the men I ever met ...

DEL.   And I'm so sorry. To have added one *iota*, in my stupid ...

DONNY.   ... in this cesspool.

DEL.   Could I ...

DONNY.   *(Pause.)* No. I don't care anymore.

DEL.   Could I talk to you? Who am I? Some poor Queen. Lives in a hotel. Some silly old Soul Who loves you.

DONNY.   Oh, please.

DEL.   No — I need you to forgive me.

DONNY.   Why would I do that?

DEL.   You should do that if it would make you happy.

DONNY.   No, look here: don't tell me I'm going to make a sacrifice for you, and it's for my own good. Do you see?

[handwritten margin note: homosexuality?]

53

Because every man I ever met in this shithole.... Don't you dare come in my house and do that. You faggot. Every man I ever met in my life ...

DEL. *Well, why does it happen?*

DONNY. Excuse me...?

DEL. Why does it happen? Is it chance? Do you think it's some mystery? What you encounter? What you provoke...?

DONNY. What I *provoke...?*

DEL. That's right.

DONNY. What are you saying?

DEL. Well ...

DONNY. You might as well say it.

DEL. Are you sure?

DONNY. Oh. Don't "tease" me ... mmm? For God's sake: don't "tease" me, lad ...

DEL. ... No.

DONNY. You came to say your little piece — go on.

DEL. All right. For some time, for quite a long time I've watched you.

DONNY. *Have* you?

DEL. I have ...

DONNY. You've *watched* me.

DEL. ... and I've thought about you. And the boy. Quite a long time.

DONNY. Well ...

DEL. All right. Here is what I think: *(Pause. John appears at the head of the stairs. Pause.)*

DONNY. Yes. Yes, John, What?

JOHN. I ...

DONNY. What? What? You promised. Did you promise?

JOHN. ... I ...

DONNY. ... It's not a small *thing*. You ...

JOHN. I only ...

DONNY. Yes, *What? What?* "You Only ..." You prom ...

JOHN. ... I only ...

DONNY. I DON'T CARE. Do You Know What It Means To Give ...

JOHN. ... I ...

DONNY. ... to give your word? I DON'T CARE.

JOHN. I ...

DONNY. I don't care. Do you hear? I don't care. You *promised* me that you would stay upstairs.

JOHN. ... I ...

DONNY. I don't care. Go away. You lied.

DEL. Donny ...

DONNY. I love you, but I can't like you.

DEL. Donny ...

DONNY. Do you know why? You lied.

DEL. Let me.... Let me ... John: Here. Go to bed. Take the book. This is the book, John. We were talking about. It was my copy. It's yours now. "That's what the Wizard said." It's yours. Off you go. If you can't sleep ...

JOHN. ... I ...

DEL. F'you can't sleep, you read it. It's all right now. You go to bed. S'all right. Off you go. *(Pause.)*

JOHN. I have to cut the twine.

DONNY. The twine.

JOHN. On the box.

DONNY. I don't understand.

JOHN. To get to the blanket. It's tied.

DEL. All right, go to the kitchen, take, no, they're packed. Are they packed? They're put away, John. The knives are put away. *(Pause.)*

JOHN. You said I could have the blanket.

DEL. Well,

JOHN. You said that.

DEL. Well, you'll have to do without. But you'll be fine, I promise you. We'll ...

DONNY. Goodnight, John.

DEL. You understand. You'll be fine. Goodnight, now.

JOHN. You said I could have the blanket.

DEL. Goodnight, Jjjj ... *(John starts to exit.)*

DONNY. John? Del said "goodnight" to you. *(Pause.)* Did you hear him?

DEL. It's all right.

DONNY. John...?

DEL.   It's alr …

DONNY.   No. It isn't all right. I'm speaking to you. Come back here. John? The man said goodnight to you. Come back down and tell the man you're sorry.

DEL.   It's all right, Donny.

DONNY.   John? I'm *speaking* to you. What must I do?

DEL.   Donn …

DONNY.   What must I do that you treat me like an animal?

DEL.   It's …

DONNY.   Don't you tell me it's all right, for the love of God. Don't you *dare* to dispute me.

DEL.   The child …

DONNY.   Don't you *dare* to dispute me in my home. Now, I'm *speaking* to you, John. Don't stand there so innocently. I've asked you a question. Do you want me to go mad? Is that what you want? Is that what you want?

DEL.   Your mother's speaking to you, John.

DONNY.   Is that what you want?

DEL.   She asked you a question.

DONNY.   Can't you see that I need comfort? Are you blind? For the love of God …   ↳ behavior of a child

JOHN.   I hear voices.

DEL.   John: Your mother's waiting for you to …

JOHN.   Before I go to sleep.

DEL.   Your mother's waiting, John. What does she want to hear?

JOHN.   … before I go to sleep.

DEL.   What does she want to hear you say?

JOHN.   I don't know.

DEL.   I think that you do. *(Pause.)* What does she want to hear you say. *(Pause.)*

JOHN.   "I'm sorry."

DEL.   What?

JOHN.   I'm sorry.

DEL.   All right, then.

JOHN.   You told me I could have the blanket.

DONNY.   Goodnight, John.

JOHN.   You told me I could have the blanket.

DEL.   Yes. You can.

JOHN.   It's wrapped up.

DEL.   Take the knife. When you're done ... *(Hands the boy the knife.)*

JOHN.   I can't fall asleep.

DEL.   That's up to you, now.

JOHN.   I hear voices. They're calling to me. *(Pause.)*

DONNY.   Yes I'm sure they are.

JOHN.   They're calling me.

DEL.   Take the knife and go.

JOHN.   They're calling my name. *(Pause.)* Mother. They're calling my name.

PROPERTY LIST

Pair of socks (JOHN)
Small framed photo
Pilot's knife (DEL)
Tea mugs (DONNY)
White envelope with letter (JOHN)
Medicine bottle with syrup (DEL)
Spoon (DEL)
Liquor bottle (DEL)
Drinking glasses (DEL)
Various packing boxes
Box (DONNY)
Tea tray with cups (DONNY)
Book (DEL)

SOUND EFFECTS

Teakettle whistle

SCENE DESIGN
"THE CRYPTOGRAM"
(DESIGNED BY JOHN LEE BEATTY FOR
AMERICAN REPERTORY THEATRE)

TO STREET

TO KITCHEN

ESCAPES

+9'-4"

+2'-0"

CHAIR

ROLLING OTTOMAN

SOFA

FLOATING CEILING

NEW PLAYS

• **SMASH by Jeffrey Hatcher.** Based on the novel, AN UNSOCIAL SOCIALIST by George Bernard Shaw, the story centers on a millionaire Socialist who leaves his bride on their wedding day because he fears his passion for her will get in the way of his plans to overthrow the British government. *"SMASH is witty, cunning, intelligent, and skillful."* –Seattle Weekly. *"SMASH is a wonderfully high-style British comedy of manners that evokes the world of Shaw's high-minded heroes and heroines, but shaped by a post modern sensibility."* –Seattle Herald. [5M, 5W] ISBN: 0-8222-1553-5

• **PRIVATE EYES by Steven Dietz.** A comedy of suspicion in which nothing is ever quite what it seems. *"Steven Dietz's ... Pirandellian smooch to the mercurial nature of theatrical illusion and romantic truth, Dietz's spiraling structure and breathless pacing provide enough of an oxygen rush to revive any moribund audience member ... Dietz's mastery of playmaking ... is cause for kudos."* –The Village Voice. *"The cleverest and most artful piece presented at the 21st annual [Humana] festival was PRIVATE EYES by writer-director Steven Dietz."* –The Chicago Tribune. [3M, 2W] ISBN: 0-8222-1619-1

• **DIMLY PERCEIVED THREATS TO THE SYSTEM by Jon Klein.** Reality and fantasy overlap with hilarious results as this unforgettable family attempts to survive the nineties. *"Here's a play whose point about fractured families goes to the heart, mind -- and ears."* –The Washington Post. *" ... an end-of-the-millennium comedy about a family on the verge of a nervous breakdown ... Trenchant and hilarious ... "* –The Baltimore Sun. [2M, 4W] ISBN: 0-8222-1677-9

• **HONOUR by Joanna Murray-Smith.** In a series of intense confrontations, a wife, husband, lover and daughter negotiate the forces of passion, lust, history, responsibility and honour. *"Tight, crackling dialogue (usually played out in punchy verbal duels) captures characters unable to deal with emotions ... Murray-Smith effectively places her characters in situations that strip away pretense."* –Variety. *"HONOUR might just capture a few honors of its own."* –Time Out Magazine. [1M, 3W] ISBN: 0-8222-1683-3

• **NINE ARMENIANS by Leslie Ayvazian.** A revealing portrait of three generations of an Armenian-American family. *" ... Ayvazian's obvious personal exploration ... is evocative, and her picture of an American Life colored nostalgically by an increasingly alien ethnic tradition, is persuasively embedded into a script of a certain supple grace ... "* –The NY Post. *"... NINE ARMENIANS is a warm, likable work that benefits from ... Ayvazian's clear-headed insight into the dynamics of a close-knit family ... "* –Variety. [5M, 5W] ISBN: 0-8222-1602-7

• **PSYCHOPATHIA SEXUALIS by John Patrick Shanley.** Fetishes and psychiatry abound in this scathing comedy about a man and his father's argyle socks. *"John Patrick Shanley's new play, PSYCHOPATHIA SEXUALIS is ... perfectly poised between daffy comedy and believable human neurosis which Shanley combines so well ... "* –The LA Times. *"John Patrick Shanley's PSYCHOPATHIA SEXUALIS is a salty boulevard comedy with a bittersweet theme ... "* –New York Magazine. *"A tour de force of witty, barbed dialogue."* –Variety. [3M, 2W] ISBN: 0-8222-1615-9

DRAMATISTS PLAY SERVICE, INC.
440 Park Avenue South, New York, NY 10016 212-683-8960 Fax 212-213-1539
postmaster@dramatists.com www.dramatists.com

NEW PLAYS

• **A QUESTION OF MERCY by David Rabe.** The Obie Award-winning playwright probes the sensitive and controversial issue of doctor-assisted suicide in the age of AIDS in this poignant drama. *"There are many devastating ironies in Mr. Rabe's beautifully considered, piercingly clear-eyed work ... "* –The NY Times. *"With unsettling candor and disturbing insight, the play arouses pity and understanding of a troubling subject ... Rabe's provocative tale is an affirmation of dignity that rings clear and true."* –Variety. [6M, 1W] ISBN: 0-8222-1643-4

• **A DOLL'S HOUSE by Henrik Ibsen, adapted by Frank McGuinness. Winner of the 1997 Tony Award for best revival.** *"New, raw, gut-twisting and gripping. Easily the hottest drama this season."* –USA Today. *"Bold, brilliant and alive."* –The Wall Street Journal. *"A thunderclap of an evening that takes your breath away."* –Time. *"The stuff of Broadway legend."* –Associated Press. [4M, 4W, 2 boys] ISBN: 0-8222-1636-1

• **THE WAITING ROOM by Lisa Loomer.** Three women from different centuries meet in a doctor's waiting room in this dark comedy about the timeless quest for beauty -- and its cost. *" ... THE WAITING ROOM ... is a bold, risky melange of conflicting elements that is ... terrifically moving ... There's no resisting the fierce emotional pull of the play."* – The NY Times. *" ... one of the high points of this year's Off-Broadway season ... THE WAITING ROOM is well worth a visit."* –Back Stage. [7M, 4W, flexible casting] ISBN: 0-8222-1594-2

• **MR. PETERS' CONNECTIONS by Arthur Miller.** Mr. Miller describes the protagonist as existing in a dream-like state when the mind is "freed to roam from real memories to conjectures, from trivialities to tragic insights, from terror of death to glorying in one's being alive." With this memory play, the Tony Award and Pulitzer Prize-winner reaffirms his stature as the world's foremost dramatist. *" ... a cross between Joycean stream-of-consciousness and Strindberg's dream plays, sweetened with a dose of William Saroyan's philosophical whimsy ... CONNECTIONS is most intriguing ... Miller scholars will surely find many connections of their own to make between this work and the author's earlier plays."* –The NY Times. [5M, 3W] ISBN: 0-8222-1687-6

• **THE STEWARD OF CHRISTENDOM by Sebastian Barry.** A freely imagined portrait of the author's great-grandfather, the last Chief Superintendent of the Dublin Metropolitan Police. *"MAGNIFICENT ... the cool, elegiac eye of James Joyce's THE DEAD; the bleak absurdity of Samuel Beckett's lost, primal characters; the cosmic anger of KING LEAR ..."* –The NY Times. *"Sebastian Barry's compassionate imaging of an ancestor he never knew is among the most poignant onstage displays of humanity in recent memory."* –Variety. [5M, 4W] ISBN: 0-8222-1609-4

• **SYMPATHETIC MAGIC by Lanford Wilson. Winner of the 1997 Obie for best play.** The mysteries of the universe, and of human and artistic creation, are explored in this award-winning play. *"Lanford Wilson's idiosyncratic SYMPATHETIC MAGIC is his BEST PLAY YET ... the rare play you WANT ... chock-full of ideas, incidents, witty or poetic lines, scientific and philosophical argument ... you'll find your intellectual faculties racing."* – New York Magazine. *"The script is like a fully notated score, next to which most new plays are cursory lead sheets."* –The Village Voice. [5M, 3W] ISBN: 0-8222-1630-2

DRAMATISTS PLAY SERVICE, INC.
440 Park Avenue South, New York, NY 10016 212-683-8960 Fax 212-213-1539
postmaster@dramatists.com www.dramatists.com